B.Y.O.B.

Building Your Own Brand

Karan Gupta

Copyright © 2021 Karan Gupta

All rights reserved

The characters and events portrayed in this book are fictitious. Any similarity to real persons, living or dead, is coincidental and not intended by the author.

No part of this book may be reproduced, or stored in a retrieval system, or transmitted in any form or by any means, electronic, mechanical, photocopying, recording, or otherwise, without express written permission of the publisher.

I dedicate this book to my mother and father who have been through thick and thin beside me to support in all my life choices.

*It takes 20 years to build a reputation and five minutes to ruin it.
If you think about that, you'll do things differently.
- Warren Buffett*

Contents

Title Page
Copyright
Dedication
Epigraph
Introduction

Branding for Designers	1
Why Branding for Designers?	11
Steps to Branding for Designers	21
Products vs. Designers	30
Brand Strategy 101	35
Building Brand Strategy	40
Listening for Your Brand	45
Your Customer's Character	48
Uncommon Denominator	52
Benefit Ladder	58
Brand's Positioning Statement	64
Brand's Character	68
Brand Assets	74
Brand Touchpoints	85
Brand Logo	95

Create a brand logo	101
Wordmark	105
Monogram	108
Icon	111
Wordmark as a brand logo.	115
Monogram as a brand logo.	119
Icon as a brand logo.	122
10 steps to create a successful brand logo.	126
Blogging for Designers	129
Bonus:101 Blog Ideas	137
Acknowledgement	147
Books By This Author	149
About The Author	157

Introduction

Who Is This Book For?

This book is tailored for professionals in the fields of graphic design, branding design, visual design, ui/ux, business administration, brand management, public relations, architecture, interior design, content marketing and communication design.

It is also an informative read for young design and business graduates or students who wish to explore the world of branding.

Lastly, this book is also crafted in a simple non-design language for people from all scores of life to explore the world of branding and how brands are established over time.

How To Read This Book?

You can skim through the entire book to find your exact interest and read it separately.

You can also read the book in a continuous flow to start by understanding the need for branding and then to creating brand assets.

What Value Will This Book Bring To You?

You'll realise branding is not just the brand logo, some business cards or your letterhead. You'll realise the amount of time and effort that goes into building a powerful brand that creates a legacy.

You'll realize that branding for products is totally different from service or design. Lastly, you'll come across some definitive actionable steps to build your own brand.

What's In The Next Series Of This Book?

This book ends at a cliffhanger note by creating brand logos but we will explore how to curate brand colors, typography, tone of voice, imagery, illustrations, iconography, patterns and a lot more in the next part.

We will also understand how brand attributes should be reflected in all the brand assets such as packaging, marketing collaterals, website, social media and more. We shall also go through a case study of establishing the brand of an architecture studio through dialogues and discussions.

Branding for Designers

Why is Branding & Marketing more important for designers today than ever before?

> *A brand for a company is like a reputation for a person. You earn reputation by trying to do hard things well.*
>
> - JEFF BEZOS

The need for designers to realize the significance of branding and marketing in today's context.

Why this Chapter? Because designers haven't been paying much attention to Branding and Marketing lately.

How will you benefit? You'll realize what you as a designer are missing out by neglecting this secret ingredient to skyrocketing your design career!

What is Branding and Marketing? What do I mean by 'for

designers'? You might've come across these two mistakenly interchangeable terms in your daily life. We've been so associated with brands these days that possessing a non-branded item is almost a shame!

In simple terms, branding is defining a strategy with mission and values that'll guide your business in the long run. It is the 'why' of your business. Marketing is the 'how' of your business.

Marketing is a micro-level short term strategy. I'll get into the understanding of these two terminologies later because you're not here for a lecture on business management.

Why are you here? You're here to walk with me through a journey wherein I'll show you how the world around us has changed since the industrial revolution, how design has evolved over the past century and how designers have been unable to cope up with branding and marketing when compared to the products they design.

This chapter hopes to evoke your emotional intelligence in understanding the necessity for a designer to establish his/her brand.

Do you remember? Do you remember the world before people around you started using the word 'design' in their everyday lives? Chances are that you might have seen that engineered era or might have heard about it from your parents.

People were constructing buildings, decorating their house interiors, inventing products, developing code, putting together a computer, setting up their website and all this time they had been engineering our lives.

This was the industrial age when the world around us was transforming to suit our basic needs with minimum concern towards user experience. In fact, people were too amazed by the technology and products serving their basic needs that they didn't mind putting in the extra effort. They called it the idiot box.

Let's take the example of the television. It allowed people to be connected to the entire world at the blink of an eye. People were too overwhelmed by its possibilities that they didn't mind if it was black and white or if one had to go up the roof and adjust the antenna to get better signals.

Computers back in the 90s didn't care about fancy fonts or easy to understand interface or voice control.

Computers were merely televisions with keyboards to type in code language until design masters such as Steve Jobs, Bill Gates, Steve Wozniak, and many more realized the need for a personal computer. This personal computer soon transformed into the smartphone everyone of us holds today.

Such developments happened over time with what we today call 'Design'.

Design Is A Mystery

Design is what makes our lives simpler and interesting. It's that secret ingredient which creates the flavour of a product. The layman doesn't understand the language of creating good design because it takes years of effort to master this craft.

Designers are special creatures gifted and prepared with an ability to identify the missing links between humans and their surroundings. They are noble men and women who make our everyday lives a bliss. They hold upon themselves huge burdens and often perceive themselves responsible for mankind's evolution. It's, in fact, true to some extent.

Soon 'Design' Became A Trend

As we stepped into the 20th century, design became a

significant part of our lives. Everyone followed the trend. From designer clothes to designer bags to designer footwear to designer shirts, clothing being our closest secondary environment was the first to take up this trend.

Soon this trend flushed the media taking in designer furniture, interiors, jewelry, stationery, private vehicles, and almost everything we were surrounded with.

The designer products were often associated with a prominent luxury brand owned by an aristocrat or a member of a royal society with an artistic flair. Most of them had no education in design or any experience. Perhaps it was never a profession.

Are you wondering why they were so successful and not the miserable potter in your neighborhood or the painter on your streets? It's because the former had mastered the art of Branding and Marketing their designs.

Design Is Not The Same Now

Fortunately, that's not how the design industry works today. There are just too many of these rich spoilt aristocrats failing every day to convince people with their useless hobbies they'd like to call 'design'. It's too much noise out there. There are too many people with a pretentious design flare.

There are too many media channels promoting designers only with words, no actions. With the advent of the digital information age, almost everyone is becoming a designer.

Remember Your Shopping Experience?

Remember how you used to shop in the 90s when you would go to a local neighborhood grocery store with a list of items handed over to by your mom. There wasn't much to choose from.

Compare it with how you visit the shopping mall today with an empty cart. You spend hours roaming around the store with ultimate freedom to choose from a million brand choices of the same product.

Which brand of tomato sauce should you buy? They don't have your regular so which one to select from these tons of shelves!? What if the new one doesn't go with your dishes? What if the new one has artificial flavours? What if the expensive one is nothing but a scam and not truly natural?

Surely, this comes with a hidden jolt of anxiety and indecisiveness.

Too Much Silent Noise Today

This scenario is comparable to the designers out there today. People today are confused and overwhelmed with a million choices when it comes to hiring a designer for a particular project.

Should he hire someone with no experience? Maybe give it to a corporate firm? Or to trust his relative's son for the design? Maybe he can copy something from Pinterest? Should he go online and hire a freelancer? What if the experienced designer is old fashioned? What if the young inexperienced designer just messes up the project? How would he know if he has to hire a specialist designer or a general consultant?

Designers, it's time for you to step out of that well.

Why Branding for Designers?

Why is 'now' the right time for your design career to adopt branding and marketing?

> Personal branding is about managing your name — even if you don't own a business — in a world of misinformation, disinformation, and semi-permanent Google records.
>
> - TIM FERRISS

Designers at any stage in their design career or journey can begin with branding and marketing. No need to wait until the axe is sharp enough. Someone might just order a chainsaw while you were busy sharpening your axe.

Why Is It Written?

Because designers tend to put off this task of branding and marketing until the 'right' time. Sadly, it's too late by then.

What's In It For You?

You're probably a designer or a good friend of one. You'll realize what you're missing out on by staying in your shell. You'll be surprised to know what can happen if you don't start now!

Who Are You And What Are You Doing With This Precious Time?

Are you currently studying design at a graduate college? Have you recently passed out of design college and are clueless about your future?

Let me guess, you've been the head of a design studio for years now and got no time for marketing? Or you're his best employee working your way through the week at a 9-5 corporate design agency?

Let me ask you something. What do you think you're doing with your precious time right now? You're probably slogging over Photoshop or sleeping over a render engine.

You're managing a design team or you're getting managed.

This chapter is meant for you. I'll pick up each one of you from the crowd and walk you through a journey of your design career.

Are You A Recent Design Graduate?

You've probably passed out of the design school or college with dreams to transform the world as we imagine today. You might be anxious and overwhelmed by what lies ahead of you.

You're thinking of applying for a 9 to 5 job at a design agency. You've got a good set of design skills but are too reluctant to put it out in the world. You wish to sharpen your skills further before you can actually start presenting quality designs to the world.

Imagine you get this job after struggling through rounds of interviews in front of businessmen who have no idea how you design stuff. Imagine you're employed as a junior designer in an elite corporate firm.

You've been waking up everyday for the past few months with one thought on your mind i.e. "Where's my own identity?!".

It must feel comfortable at times when you get to enjoy the weekends by partying late till night. It must be amazing when you get the paycheck at the same time every month.

Now imagine the worst-case scenario. For some unfortunate reason, you've got to leave the job before sufficient experience. You were still in your probation period.

You have got no experience letter to show ahead. You're not allowed to take the designs you worked on because of privacy reasons. You know you've got the talent. But does the world know?

How do you get ahead in these unfortunate times? How do you cope up with such situations in the beginning of your design career?

Are You A Senior Employee At A Design Agency?

What have you sacrificed till now for your corporate job? Your time and skill for the upliftment of a corporation or a narcissistic boss?

Was it all worth it? You've probably spent the last 5 to 10 years at your job. You're their best employee. You've grown a comfort bubble around you.

So, you never thought of developing your own brand or market yourself out there. You thought you might betray the company which gives your family insurance and other candies to stick to your sweet spot in the office.

Imagine you get laid off.

Now imagine you wake up tomorrow to get ready for the last Friday of the month when all you've got to do is spend a few hours reviewing the week's work and go home with a paycheck to party on!

Instead, your boss calls up in the morning to inform you that you've been laid off from the company for some reason. Your best morning turns into your worst nightmare. You come back home with all your office stuff and without the paycheck. But you were their best employee!?

How do you pull yourself together now? Nobody knows about you. How will you get another job? You're thinking of starting your own design practice but how will you get clients?

You're too old for job hunting now. Do you stay back at home? Do you apply at a design college to teach students? But how do you present yourself?

Suddenly you regret not setting up your own brand and market yourself in the past 10 years while working at the corporate job. Fear not. Let me pinch you. It's just a bad dream you've got to wake up from!

Imagine you get promoted.

Now imagine another bittersweet situation. You wake up tomorrow morning with a surprise email from your company.

It goes like,"Dear Whatever Your Name Is, sadly our current CEO has been arrested after being found guilty in a drug case. So, congratulations, you're the new CEO of our design agency. Good luck".

You're both excited and terrified at the same time. You've always been standing behind your boss in meetings. You have no contacts of your own.

The clients don't really get along with you because they've no idea how good you are. The clients always thought it was your boss who came up with brilliant ideas.

So, how do you keep his legacy and business running? Do you accept the challenge or throw the ball at someone else to be the champion? Maybe you realize the importance of Branding and

Marketing now?

Do you regret not working on your own brand again? Don't worry. Let me pinch you again. It's just another bittersweet nightmare I've been showing you.

Are You The Leader Of A Small Design Studio?

You love to micromanage your design studio. You've been managing your beloved design team since the day they were your college mates. You're passionate about your work.

You begin and end the day with design discussions. You spend hours everyday on calls with clients running away with your fees, consultants requesting their fees, potential clients asking for another design change and what not.

You're tired of the incessant complaints from your clients who don't understand the beauty of minimalism and your employees who called in sick today. You're frustrated with the silly design interns who believe Photoshop will solve all your problems.

Imagine your run out of business.

All this while branding and marketing has been the last priority on your business plan. But let's say you've fallen in love with your project.

What if it gets nowhere? What if there's not much funding available and the clients decide to take down the project? Your dreams are shattered. You're heartbroken now. All that hard work was in vain. Your design skills were of no use. So, any call from the last client you were in touch with? What about new projects?

You never cared about your image and now your entire design team will have to suffer the consequences of your neglect.

How do you take the business forward? Do you regret not investing enough time and money in branding and marketing before this tragedy? Do you draw down the shutter of your studio or do you rise from the ashes?!

Fear not. This was the last nightmare I had to show you tonight to strike fear in your mind i.e. the fear of missing out.

'Right now' is the right time!

We've gone through the scenarios where designers put off

branding and marketing until tomorrow only to realize the blunder they've made.

You've probably heard of traditional businesses and products such as cable television, music box, digital cameras, photo booths, etc. go out of date.

But designers can be lost if there's no one to hire them. A designer's true purpose is to solve problems of everyday life in a creative manner. And without the world being aware of such designers, how would it benefit anyone of them.

So, it doesn't really matter at what stage you're in your design career, you can and should begin the adventure of branding and marketing of your design skills or studio.

Believe me, it will save you from all the complaints in the coming future such as, "I would've made a better design. He's not even a trained designer. Ahh, look at those awful color combinations. He's got no sense of proportion. He's using a comic sans font on that banner. Look at that ugly building.

This website has got no design. The landscape here is so weird. The city is so chaotic, there's no urban design. On top of all this bullshit design, he's getting the national award by the president for that ugly building.

Why can't they hire better designers these days? Why doesn't anyone realize good design talent?!"

The intention behind the above chapter was to initiate an introductory realization amongst designers to be aware of what they're losing out on by putting off branding and marketing for their design skills.

Steps to Branding for Designers

11 simple steps for designers to begin with branding and marketing

If people believe they share values with a company, they will stay loyal to the brand.

- HOWARD SCHULTZ

The first step is the toughest of all. We, designers, very well fear this syndrome of starting design. In this chapter, I've created a simple yet informative process of beginning with branding and marketing as if you've never touched it before. The process may vary with design fields and years of practice but the basic laws of nature don't change.

The following are the 11 simplified steps to initiate your branding adventure!

Identify What You're Good At!

Take out the notepad and list down your design strengths. If you're inexperienced, you might be unsure of your skills but believe me, you must be good at something. Take a few deep breaths and make an exhaustive list of what you or your company does the best.

Are you experts in a particular category of design? Do your clients trust you for your efficiency? Look back at your history.

Probably your philosophy is quite unique? Do you excel at communicating your design solutions? Are you working with the latest technology available?

List down your Unique Selling Points. Consider yourself or your company as a product out in the market. Why do you think the customer will buy you?

What value can you provide to your customers through your designs? Strive to answer such questions and you'll realize your worth.

Collect, Search And Dig In!

We, designers, tend to crumble our designs and toss them in a dustbin as soon as we get over them. Next time, just don't do this! At this stage, you need to dig into your old work.

Search for those discarded sketches, those archived attempts, old photographs, and whatever that is related to your project. Much like a detective you need to collect as much evidence as you can to solve the mystery.

This task needs to be taken seriously! I know once we get over a design we don't even look back. But believe me, to move ahead you need your design history.

Go look in your servers, search your hard-disk, ask your colleagues and clients. Get that project documented if you haven't till now!

Discuss It With Your Team!

The people who have been in the design journey alongside you deserve to be a part of this adventure. Discuss it with your team. What do they think of their company and how it has grown over the years?

If you're a newbie, go ask your friends about your design journey. They might give an interesting perspective you might've missed. Sometimes, others know us better than ourselves.

Believe me, it'll be an insightful exercise. Moreover, your colleagues or employees or friends will feel that they're going to be a part of something big.

Extract The Brand Values!

Brand values are the filtered outcomes of the above steps. They're much like the pulpy juice after grinding the oranges. They are the words or phrases that have been guiding and will be guiding your brand in the future.

They need to be simple, clear, elegant, and evocative. Simple to make it punchy. Clear to make it comprehensible by your audience. Elegant to make it flow beautifully. Evocative to make it stimulating and to evoke an emotion amongst your audience and teams.

Amateur brands lack the above qualities by being pretentious about who they are and what they do. While deciding brand values, it's necessary to focus on what is, not what it wants to be.

Stick The Brand Values On A Wall!

Yes, stick them on every wall in your office, studio, home, and desktop. Remind yourself of these values every day. Make them the holy verses. Be obsessed with these values and let your employees be too! You're all now on a single train towards a single destination.

Design Your Brand Identity.

Begin with designing your identity through some basic assets such as brand name, brand logo, brand tagline, color scheme, and typography.

You can either get them designed through someone else or better yet make them yourself to avoid the fuss of explaining yourself to an external agency. You're a designer, you probably have better design sense. If you're not a visual designer then consult branding companies or designers and make sure your intentions are reflected in the identity.

Set a deadline for this task as it can take forever. These are basic identifies of your brand. You don't need to spend years perfecting a logo or coming up with a tagline. These are momentary and can be changed with time.

Brainstorm with your team and get it over with. Remember, Apple computers began with a rainbow color logo and now it's silver. These can change over time but just don't commit the mistake of over-doing or over-spending time, money and effort on these assets.

Get A Website Already!

Newborn babies have their own websites nowadays! Dogs and Cats have their own website nowadays! The world has gone digital now. Your design career should also!

A website offers you a limitless, interactive and global platform to show yourself to the world. It's a one-time investment into a portfolio that'll serve your branding and marketing for many years.

I'll be explaining how to set up a modern website with your works and services in upcoming books. But I believe there's a lot of content on how to set up one.

It doesn't even require you to know to code. So, what are you waiting for? Are you waiting for your domain name to be stolen by someone else?!

Set Up Your Social Media Accounts!

Facebook is outdated but still a good pass time. Instagram is trendy but there's limitless scrolling of photos.

Pinterest has been your source of inspiration for a long time. YouTube has been full of cat videos and your source of daily entertainment.

But these social media platforms are no longer restricted to entertainment. The entire world is engrossed in such media platforms and thus it serves as the best kind of marketing tool.

Although each one of them has its own strategy which I'll be discussing in further posts. But the key is consistency to gain content engagement.

Spread The Word!

Share! Announce your brand establishment to everyone you know. Text your colleagues about it. Email your contacts surprising them with this achievement. Call your relatives and explain your brand to them. Talk about it as much as you can. Just don't stay silent and expect a Ginnie to do the work for you!

Take Further Steps To Branding Design!

Now after a few months of spreading your brand amongst the public, you can take the next step to advanced Branding. It includes taking the next step towards strengthening your brand language and reach.

It requires you to invest in long term goals such as e-mail marketing through Newsletters, compiling your work in a publication, pitching magazines and journals to publish your work, creating more brand assets such as presentations, portfolio, letterheads, reports, etc, and setting up interior space branding.

There's the next step to online marketing which includes paid publicity and hiring an SEO marketer.

But these tasks should always be achieved step by step. Remember, branding and marketing happen over a long period of time. You can't expect to be famous overnight. Go rob a bank if you want that!

Have patience, consistency and engagement!

All this is an exciting adventure in the beginning when you'll be building your brand. But when you find yourself anxiously waiting for more website views or more Instagram followers or more likes, calm yourself down. Rome wasn't built in a day.

Just don't commit the mistake of inconsistency as your work absorbs you again. Remember, in this digital age, everything is temporary and so is your visibility out there. You'll be forgotten if you stop running your branding activities.

∞∞∞

Products vs. Designers

3 reasons why branding for designers is different from that of Products

> A brand is a voice and a product is a souvenir.
>
> - LISA GANSKY

You designers might be wondering why you need a different approach towards branding and marketing. You might have gone through a lot of marketing advice out there. You must have read a lot of books on branding and marketing strategies.

But you still aren't convinced with the approach. This article is for all the designers who wish to know the reason why typical product marketing just won't work for your design career.

Product Vs Process

You're trying to sell a process, not a product. By offering your design services you're selling a much more insightful and intellectual story than material or immaterial product. It's more complex than it sounds.

Your design process is a secret of yours only. It is a skill that you've mastered over years of practice. It's nothing like a sharp axe. It's you!

You are not a product that people can use and throw. You just don't sit on the shopping mall's shelf silently waiting to be picked by a customer. You cannot be returned and resold in the market. So, why do you fall into the trap of adopting Branding and Marketing techniques made specifically for products?!

You need to sell your process. You need to brand your skills. You must market your intellect. You should inform people about what they're missing out by not hiring you.

You have the one thing no product has. You've attained a voice. You're full of empathy. You've got the ability to seduce your clients. You have the power to show them dreams.

Above all, you've got the ability to interact! So, ditch all the traditional branding and marketing norms and pave your own path.

Typical Marketing Agencies Don't Understand Designers

If you're a designer, you've probably had the trouble of explaining what you do to almost everyone.

In the last couple of years, I've seen many designers struggle in explaining themselves to typical product marketing agencies. It simply doesn't work out well.

The major reason behind this misunderstanding and frustration is that designers spend an enormous time on developing their design skills. They spend years of practice in design schools and then years in the field trying to convince the world of their designs.

How can one possibly inject this kind of adventure into a marketing agency in a couple of days? And expect them to comprehend the designers' minds?!

I have one piece of advice for such struggling designers knocking the doors of marketing agencies. Just stop putting in the double effort.

Stop wasting your time in explaining yourself to someone who pretends who understands it and market in place of you. You'd be a rather better person to do so by yourself.

Designers Help Sell Others' Products But Who Sells Them?

Graphic designers help businesses sell their products by creating exciting visuals. Architects help developers sell their buildings to potential clients.

Web designers help companies to set up their online presence in order to enhance their business reach. Brand designers help companies establish their brand through brand assets.

All this while designers focus on creating business for their clients. But what about themselves? Who will sell them? How do they help their own business?

Designers need to realize the significance of personal branding while they help others' businesses. It's not a charity. Designers are not super-rich people giving out their skills for free. They need help with their business too.

Conclusion

So, it's pretty clear why designers should wipe off the burden of hiring external agencies to take up their marketing tasks. Now, I'm not suggesting to give up your design career and spend most of the time establishing your brand yourself. This can be harmful to your own health.

Currently, there are many external agencies specializing in branding and marketing exclusively for designers. One just needs to search for such hidden mascots and take their help.

All I'm trying to convey is that designers are way different from products on a shelf and it's high time that these designers get themselves out in the public. By themselves. Period.

Brand Strategy 101

What designers need to know about brand strategy?

A brand is the set of expectations, memories, stories and relationships that, taken together, account for a consumer's decision to choose one product or service over another.

- SETH GODIN

Brand is like the word 'India'. It can mean so many things at the same time, all of them vastly different from one and other. If you say 'India' while you're envisioning New Delhi while your listeners envision 'Mumbai'. It's not going to be a very productive conversation.

A brand is the same word. When I say 'Brand' some people will think of a funky logo, while others will think of a brand name or social media; other advertising. All these and many more are components of a brand but not a brand strategy.

A brand strategy allows you to use all such brand components in a concentrated, focused, and thoughtful way such that you're defining the business; not letting it be defined by the surrounding market.

So, how do you differentiate your brand?

You deliberately create a brand strategy. And this is what this series of articles is all about.

I want to help you use your brand as a catalyst for growing a meaningful business. With a deliberate brand strategy, you can assure that you're focusing your time, energy, and your money on the stuff that is most closely aligned with your north star i.e. your brand strategy.

What Is A Brand?

Before beginning on the quest of brand strategy, allow me to first explain to you, what a brand is?

The brand is one of these crazy words that gets used so broadly that sometimes it's really hard to know what someone really means when they hear the word 'Brand'.

So, What Exactly Is A Brand?

The brand comes from the old Norse word brandr which means "to burn". People would burn into their cattle or to their belongings. Something to signify their ownership. Over time it came to mean "I own it so therefore I stand by its quality. And you should pay more for it."

So, your brand can manifest in infinite ways from your logo to your advertising, imagery, product, service, buying experience. In all those cases, your brand: Communicates what business stands for; Relationship between your business and audience; Result of everything you do.

Now, since brand is the result of everything you do, How do we make it powerful?

We do so by deliberately choosing our brands' optimal position, it's the optimal meaning and letting that choice guide everything we do to build our business.

What Is A Brand Strategy?

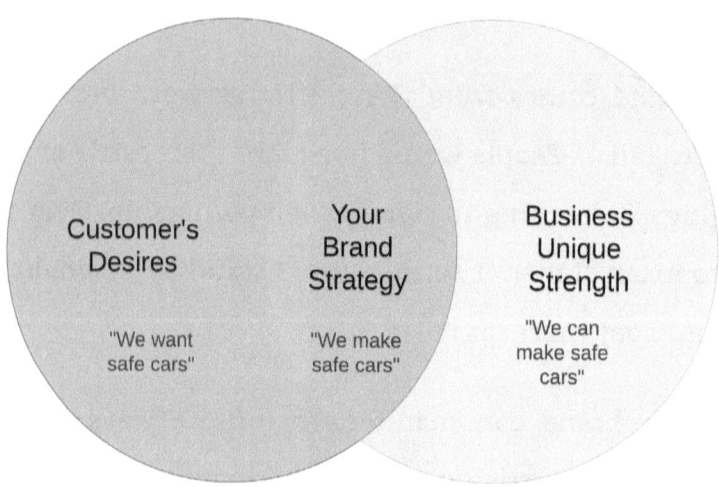

Brand strategy is this deliberate exercise of choosing your brand's optimal position. It's an exercise of deliberately accessing where you best fit in your customer's world. What is the position you seek to own in your customers' mind?

When done well, your brand strategy is an overlap of your customers' desires and the unique strength of your business.

For example, Volvo's customer's desire was 'safety' which overlapped with the unique strength of actually making safe automobile vehicles allowing them to create this as their brand strategy. With this, Volvo now makes all the decisions based on their north star of 'safety'.

This exercise of deliberately creating your brand positioning is important because all brand positions are not all equally attractive. "Position or be positioned", as they say. If you don't go through the exercise to articulate your brand character carefully and use actual customer insights and actual insights about your own business. Then you'll have a positioning but it will likely not be the most beneficial to you.

Building Brand Strategy

How to build a successful Brand Strategy?

Products are made in a factory but brands are created in the mind.
— WALTER LANDOR

Well, the first thing we need to do is to frame the strategy. But before that, we need to prepare for this exercise.

We'll define the target customer and the competitive frame of reference and then you'll schedule your customer interviews. Then you'll prepare questions for those interviews.

Define Your Target Customer/Audience

So, first you define your target customer. Who is your sweet spot customer? Some Ways to define this question:

Identify a uniting theme. What do they all have in common?;

Explore who you benefit the most. To whom do you bring disproportionate value?; Determine who brings your business the most value?; Who are the people who bring disproportionate value to you?; Zoom out and consider your mission. Why are you in business? Who is the person you've created your business to serve?

Allow me to give you an example. Say I'm a company 'XYZ' which markets outdoor gear and apparels online in retail stores across the world. Our mission is not only to have a healthy bottom line but also to get more people to nurture and enjoy the great outdoors.

Our best customers, who bring us the most value and who, we bring the most value are the outdoor enthusiasts. They spend the most with us and by embracing the outdoors, they are also helping with our mission to cultivate environmental stewardship.

Allow me to give you another example, this time, of an Architecture Design consultancy named 'ABC', which specializes in two fields i.e. Institutional designs and utilizing Building Information Modelling.

Their mission is not only to design better spaces for the universities but also to efficiently execute their design ideas through the latest technology. Their best customers or clients who bring them the most value and who, they bring the most value to, are the Institution organizations who wish to execute their buildings without any hassle.

They help with their mission of better architecture design for the young generations along with the adaptation of the latest technology in Architecture Design.

Define Your Competitive Frame Of Reference

The second step is to identify your true competitor. You're asking your target customer to buy your offering instead of what exactly? It could be a direct competitor; Substitute; Workaround something completely different from what you're offering.

If I go back to the example of the company 'XYZ'. I'll say our competitor is other retailers that sell outdoor wear. They range from specialist retailers such as Woodland, Quechua to general retailers such as Amazon and Walmart.

If I talk about the same Architecture Design consultancy named 'ABC'. I'll say their competitors are other Architecture Design studios specializing in Institutional designs. And the Real estate companies with a specialization in executing buildings with the latest technology.

Schedule Customer Interviews

So, now you're ready to schedule some customer/client interviews. There are lots of ways in which you can conduct these interviews.

It can be in small focused groups that you conduct or hire a facilitator to conduct.

It could be a pizza party that you invite your sweet spot customers to. Maybe over coffee.

My personal favorite way is to set up 30-40 minute phone calls with each of these individuals. Sometimes the person on the other end feels safe if someone else is not listening to their responses. Also, it saves time.

Create An Interview Guide

The last step is to make a list of questions that you'll be using to interview your customers. Whichever setting you choose, you're going to get in front of your customers and have. What people in the design thinking world would like to call, Empathy

Interviews.

This is the way to get inside the world of your sweet spot customers. So that you can view your business and brand development from the customers' standpoint. Outside in, rather than Inside out.

There are lots of ways to structure this interview. But I like to do it to start at a high altitude and then narrow down. Start very general and then narrow it down to your offering and your brand.

That way you'll get a more realistic view as to how you fit in the context. And it's more true to the customers' actual way of thinking.

Listening for Your Brand

How listening can help you build a strong brand strategy?

> *Your brand is the single most important investment you can make in your business.*
>
> — STEVE FORBES

By listening, and listening well, you can get more precise, more meaningful, and therefore more powerful as you articulate your brand.

Remember, the purpose of brand positioning is to make it easier for your customer or client to buy. And so, listening is the step that helps us in getting the raw data to help us do this.

The Listening Mindset

You have to be truly open.

You need to be genuine.

You must be non-judgemental.

You ought to be curious.

This can be hard and sometimes it's not a bad idea to bring in an outside party to do the interview for you. Even if you do that you still need to have a genuine curiosity for your customer.

True curiosity is not attached to the outcome. It's genuinely wanting to know more. The biggest curiosity killer is to think that you have all the answers.

Act like a reporter! Ask open-ended and expansive questions. Be open to what you hear! Being open to hearing can be uncomfortable, even humbling.

If you're not approaching your customers with vulnerability, it's highly unlikely that you'll be open enough to hear the big ideas. There are chances that you'll get a confirmation of the things you already know.

The Beginner's Mind

You want to maintain what the Zen buddhas call 'The beginner's mind'. Be open to what emerges without being attached to a certain result.

Once you're conducting your interviews, keep asking, 'Why?' and 'What about that matters to you?'

'Is there anything else?'

'What is important to you here?'.

Ask 'why' to avoid, until you've gotten to the root.

At the basics of great brands is genuine curiosity and humility. This is not the time for you to be the smartest person in the room. Feeling attached to the 'knowing' state will prevent you from truly listening.

∞∞∞

Your Customer's Character

How understanding your customer's character helps in building your brand strategy?

> *If people like you they will listen to you, but if they trust you, they'll do business with you.*
>
> — ZIG ZIGLAR

You need to understand that your customer is not going to give you all the answers. You need to do the work here.

Write a description of your target customer that taps into that customers' deeply held beliefs and values. This description can then serve as a touchstone for new and old marketing initiatives.

If you do all the research that led up to this point but you don't compile it into a digestible summary, it's easy for it to get lost in that day to day shuffle.

It's also difficult for you to share it with your teams when it's all in your head or scribbled here and there. So, take some time now to distill what you've collected into nuggets for future reference.

Demographics

Start by describing the basics of your business's ideal customer. Who is this person? Start with a basic demographic profile like age, income, gender, ethnicity, etc. and then expand on it. Any other notable type of your customer, note that now.

Psychographics

Spend some time getting inside your target customer's head. What are their attitudes and aspirations? What are their worries and scarcities in life? How do they think about themself?

Behavior

Marketing is about influencing behavior. In particular, it's about instigating a behavior to purchase or hire.

In order to do this, you need to know your customer's baseline behavior. Also, you need to understand why your customer behaves that way.

For example, how, when, and where does your customer use your product or service? What instigates their thinking about it or using it?

How, when, and where does your offering fit into the context of your customer's stay? Is it an afterthought? Do they plan it or do they avoid it? Or do they embrace it?

Beliefs

Because behaviors are rooted in beliefs, we are well served to understand underlying beliefs so that we can better influence behaviors. Identifying your customer's belief system will help you understand what makes them tick.

Where your brand fits into that and therefore how to talk about it and deliver your offerings to them.

This initial step of framing your strategy will help build a strong foundation for a powerful brand strategy.

The more thoughtful and honest you are at this stage, the granular, nuanced, and sharp-edged your brand strategy can become. The more hard-working it'll be in guiding your business growth.

Uncommon Denominator

A secret framework to build a powerful brand strategy

> Brand is the sum total of how someone perceives a particular organization. Branding is about shaping that perception.
>
> - ASHLEY FRIEDLEIN

There's this framework called the 'Uncommon Denominator Framework'.

What this framework does is that it synthesizes what we know about the customer's desires, what we know about our competitor and what they're good at; and what we know about our own strengths.

The Uncommon Denominator Framework

Right now we are in a really good position because we've gathered our insights. So, we can answer these questions from the customer's point of view.

I'd like to think of the uncommon denominator as a three-set Venn diagram. We're going to inventory everything that goes into each.

First, you're going to list the customer's desires. Now, some of these things will be actually overt, what they actually said to you. Some of it will be you reading in between the lines about what you heard. What are those insights?

Next, you're going to list your competitor's strengths. Remember your competitor could be a direct competitor but it also could be a substitute. You could be competing against behavior or a status quo or an adjacent type of product.

Again, channeling your customer, what your customer would think about, what is compelling about your competitor. List those things in the second circle in the right.

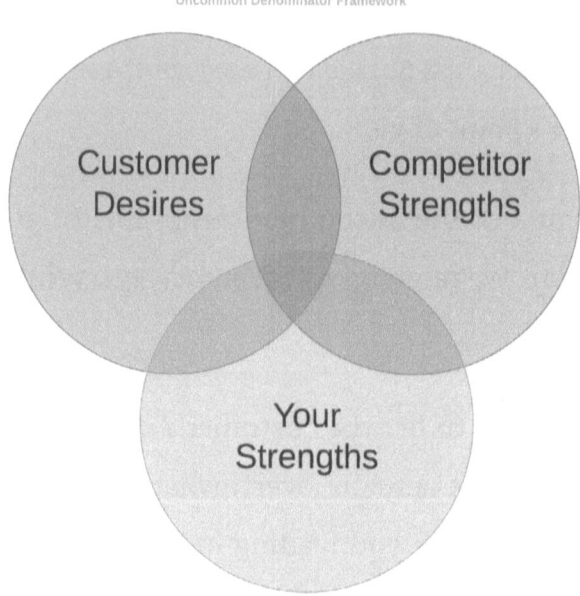

The Common Denominator

Lastly, we're going to list the things that we are good at. We can list all of the things that we know. But have a special eye towards the things that your customer expressed as your strengths. List all of these things in this third circle at the bottom.

Now, we have a combination of what our customer wants, what our competitors are good at, and what we are good at. Here is this powerful framework really helpful. There are two intersections we're interested in.

First is the very center of the Venn diagram which we call the 'Common Denominator'. These are your category benefits. Basically, the things that are important to our customers, our competitor's good and that we're good at.

These are things that are important but are table stacks. It's something you offer just by the virtue of saying that you're in this category.

So, if you make a pancake mix, your table stacks benefit is that your pancakes are delicious.

The important thing to note here is that the common denominator is useful but it's not the end of the story. It's kind of like the beginning of the story. Yes, we have to do that but we don't get to stop there.

This is probably the single biggest error that I've observed in brand strategy i.e. mistaking your table stakes benefits something you truly own.

Find Your Uncommon Denominator!

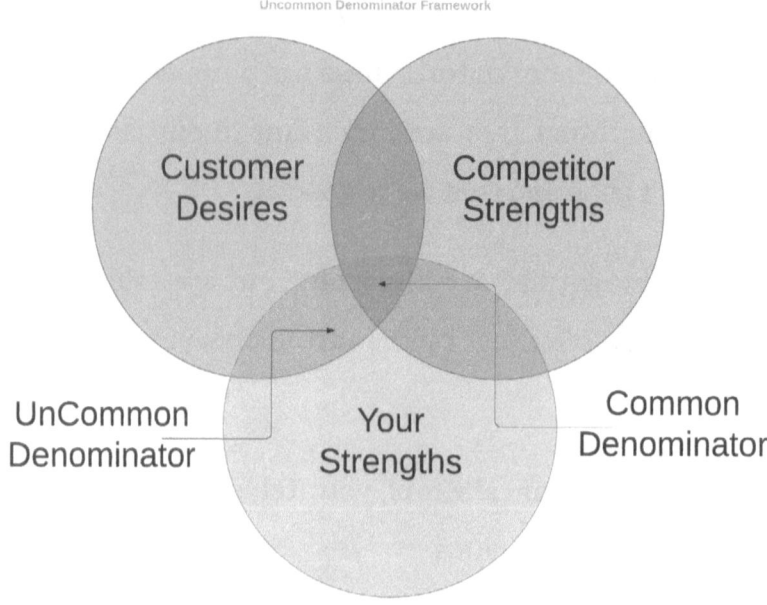

Now, let's move on from that to the uncommon denominator. It's that overlap of what your customer desires, what you're good at, and what your competitor is not good at. That is the crux of your brand positioning

So, if you're a pancake brand and you're so excited because your pancakes are so delicious, don't congratulate yourself, because you're a pancake. You should be delicious! Move on to what you uniquely bring to the table!

Similarly, if you're a designer and you design good looking stuff. Don't brag about it. You're a designer, you should be designing good looking stuff! Identify what else you bring value to! Your uncommon denominator is what you uniquely bring to the table.

So, for example, your pancake is a thin, crispy pancake that uses your Swedish grandmother's recipe. That is your uncommon denominator.

Similarly, if you're a designer and you use the latest technology to speed up the delivery process, you design stuff using sustainable materials, you communicate your design well and you stick to your client until the design is handed over. That's your uncommon denominator.

The power of your brand strategy stems from how meaningful it is to your customers or clients. And, how unique it is to you! The Venn diagram helps you to be very clear on that overlap so that you're building your positioning from this powerful foundation.

∞∞∞

Benefit Ladder

How a secret benefit ladder can help build your brand strategy?

Your brand is a gateway to your true work.

- DAVE BUCK

Proctor and Gamble launched bounce dryer sheets in 1975. Prior to that, there was no such thing as dryer sheets. So, they launched this brand new type of product with a functional benefit of wrinkle-free clothes. Because these bounce dryer sheets contained wrinkle relaxing ingredients, you put them in a dryer and voila, your clothes are wrinkle-free.

At launch, bounce promised their customers wrinkle-free clothes. For several years, wrinkle-free was the functional benefit that they messaged in all of their communications. So, a few years into their launch, customers readily understood that bounce brought them the benefit of clothes that are wrinkle-free.

Functional Benefit To Emotional Benefit

With that benefit of wrinkle-free solidified, bounce laddered up the functional benefit to a higher-order benefit of attractive clothes. Now the customer hears that bounce makes their clothes attractive. And the reason they believe that promise is that they already know that bounce makes their clothes wrinkle-free.

Notice how, what was previously the promise i.e. wrinkle-free clothes, now serves as a reason to believe in the higher-order benefit of attractive clothes.

Bounce then owned this higher-order meaning in customers' minds. And then, several years later when customers readily grasped that bounce makes their clothes attractive, bounce laddered up again.

This time with an emotional benefit of feeling pretty i.e. with bounce you can feel pretty. Why? Because your clothes look attractive.

The Benefit Ladder

This benefit ladder enables you a reality check of what is meaningful and believable to your customer audience given with where you are in your relationship with your audience.

You need to be honest with yourself about how emotional your audience will let you be about your brand. If bounce had launched with the message of 'feel pretty' even before people knew what dryer sheets were, it would've been confusing and disengaging.

So, the ladder helps you ensure not overstepping with your customer by promising so big that they won't believe it or won't understand.

The ladder also helps you to see where you're going, how are you going to keep delivering an ever larger, ever more emotional benefit.

Reasons To Rise Up?

Why is it good to deliver an ever larger, more emotional benefit? Why should you never rest on your laurels and deliver a functional benefit, without pushing it upward on this ladder? There are a few reasons.

Profit Margin

The very first reason is your profit margin. The larger and the more emotional benefit that you bring, the more customers are willing to pay for your offering, and the healthier your margins will be. People are willing to pay more to feel pretty than for an electrostatic cloth drenched in some chemicals.

Competitive Moat

The second reason is your competitive moat. The higher on this ladder is your brand's position, the more difficult it is for others to copy. It's easy to copy an ingredient but it's hard to copy with credibility a promise of feeling pretty.

Headroom To Grow

The third reason is the headroom to grow. The higher of the ladder you are, the more categories you can play in, the more you can grow laterally. If you own the promise of 'feeling pretty', you can go into categories outside of dryer sheets. So, your room for growth is more spacious.

Build Your Benefit Ladder

So, now it's time to build your benefit ladder. I advise by starting with the bottom of the ladder, with your functional benefit. What is that functional benefit your customers will most enjoy if they chose your offering? What are the factual reasons they should believe that benefit?

Now look at the next step on your ladder. What does that functional benefit enable for your customer at a bigger, more emotional level? Because of that functional benefit, how is her day better?

And lastly what is that highest order benefit, that most emotional benefit, that ultimately your customer enjoys because they purchased your product? Because of you, how is her life better?

Brand's Positioning Statement

Here's a quick way to write your brand's positioning statement

> *Your personal brand is a promise to your clients... a promise of quality, consistency, competency, and reliability.*
>
> — JASON HARTMAN

Your positioning statement captures all of your actions towards creating a brand strategy in just one distilled statement. It shows for yourself and for your teams and for your partners, the essence of your brand's position.

I recommend that you start this by putting it into plain words and answer these questions.

Identify Your Target Customer

Who is your target customer? So, for a Swedish pancake business, my target customer will be 'moms with kids at home'.

Create An Identity

What is the name of your brand? For a pancake business it can be 'Batter Pancakes'.

A Frame Of Reference Or Category

What is your customer's frame of reference? My target customer is considering us verses other pancake businesses.

What's Your Promise?

What is your brand promise? Our unique promise is that we bring 'Swedish deliciousness'.

Why Should They Believe You?

What are your reasons to believe? Our customers can believe our promise because our pancakes are super thin, pack a crispy crunch, and use my Swedish grandma's recipe.

What's Their Reward?

What is the customer's end reward for having chosen your brand? Because our customer has chosen batter pancakes, her family can start the weekend with the extraordinary.

Here's what this example looks like in a brand positioning statement.

To moms with kids at home, Batter Pancakes is the one pancake mix that brings Swedish deliciousness. That's because only Batter Pancakes brings super thin pancakes with a crispy crunch, using our Swedish grandmother's recipe so that your family can start their weekend with extraordinary.

Brand Positioning Template

Now, do this for your business. Answer the above questions and then put them into this positioning statement format.

To (your target customers), (your brand name) is the one (your frame of reference or category) that (brand promise). That's because only (your brand's name) brings (reasons to believe), so that (your target customers) can (end reward).

Once you have this brand positioning statement, congratulate yourself! You've defined the crux of your brand's position.

Brand's Character

What's a brand's character?

If you don't give the market the story to talk about, they'll define your brand's story for you.

— DAVID BRIER

Human beings connect better with people than they do with amorphous concepts. So, knowing that, we articulate our brand as to what it is as a person.

How they show up? How do they talk? That allows us to apply this style when interacting with our customers with everything we do from our messaging to imagery to our product experience.

Our brand character is another way for us to bond with our customers. It's another source of differentiation. So let's take this up.

How To Define The Brand's Character?

The first step, when defining our brand's character, is to identify our character archetype. We are hardwired to connect with stories.

You may be familiar with Carl Jung, the Swiss psychologist. He was a student of Freud and he studied storytelling across time and culture.

While studying stories, he found that there were only a handful of stories that have ever been told amongst humans.

Also, there are only a handful of characters who have ever shown up in those stories. He identified 12 total characters and he called them the character archetypes.

I'll go through what the character archetypes are, but to tie this back to branding and marketing. So, marketing experts took this Jung's character archetype idea and applied it to brands. It turns out that the great brands of the world tend to be one of these 12 character archetypes.

Carl Jung's Archetypes

The 12 character archetypes are as follows:

The Innocent

The Orphan

The Hero

The Jester

The Lover

The Caregiver

The Ruler

The Sage

The Explorer

The Rebel

The Creator

The Magician

Why Define Brands Using Archetypes?

There are two reasons that I like to start with a character archetype when defining our brand's character.

It's practical.

The first is that it is practical. Defining your brand's character can be such an overwhelming, nebulous idea. Why not let mythology do some of the work for us to help us narrow it down?!

It's a source of differentiation.

The second reason is that it's another source of differentiation. If your category, the types of brands that you compete with, are all one primary archetype. You can zag while the other zig by showing up as a different archetype.

For example, if you're a Starbucks in the 1970s, most coffee shops are either the caregiver or the lover archetype. So, Starbucks really pushed far away from that and showed up as the explorer archetype. So the first thing you're gonna do is going to just review these archetypes.

How To Define Brands Using Archetypes?

See, if there's an archetype that just feels it's your business. If you're not able to instinctively narrow down your archetype here are some steps to help you out.

Review Your Insights.

Go back to the phase when you just listened to your customers and you identified the key themes and insights. Then look at your competitors and identify what brand characters do your competitors imbibe.

Channel Your Customer.

Secondly, go back to your insights, think, and channel your customer. Consider yourself in their shoes. If your business were a person, a character in your customer story, what character archetype does your business play?

Check With Your Business' Story

Third, check with your own business's story. Do you have an instinctive feeling about what character your business plays?

Name Your Archetype.

Know that if you're still having trouble selecting your archetype, there are some standard tests out there on the web. Google 'Jung's archetype test' and there are a number of publically available tests for you.

At the end of the day, knowing your brand's archetype makes it easier to organize your brand's meaning.

And communicate it so that everyone is bringing to life your brand in a consistent and congruent way. Also, it helps you to differentiate, to not be the category cliche.

Brand Assets

How to begin with creating brand assets?

> *Brand is just a perception, and perception will match reality over time.*
>
> - ELON MUSK

Before we embark on the exciting journey of creating some amazing brand assets such as logo, colour palette, typography styles, and more; we need to absorb the reason behind these activities.

Branding is often misunderstood as this stage of creating brand assets. People generally think of a brand's logo or it's colour style when they hear the word branding. The reason why we create brand assets is not to set up our website or get some content to put on our communications.

Branding is not a solution to a broken business but a catalyst to a great business or service.

So, before even thinking of creating a brand, one should focus on creating a good business or service and ultimately a good relationship with the clients.

It's not to be done for the sole reason that everyone else is doing it so we should also have our own brand.

The major reason why we strive towards creating our brand assets is to give a practical form to our intangible brand strategy, our brand positioning statement and our brand's mission and values. This is the most important exercise to be conducted by everyone who wishes to create his or her own brand.

This activity may take up some time and effort from your end to extract the true essence of your brand but believe me, this evocative exercise of creating a brand will ensure all your marketing efforts are streamlined in the future business endeavours.

The Ultimate Realization

One of the biggest blunders committed by most budding or flawed businesses with energetic yet unfocused leaders is that they skip the exercises of creating their brand strategy. They quickly hire a graphic designer to pull out some magic trick options of logos, colour schemes and other brand assets. They chose the ones which appeal to their immediate attention and go on with hustling on their business.

Soon they realize that all of their branding and marketing activities are falling apart. None of the efforts seem to be coherent or aiding the business in any possible way.

Some clients are receiving communication in one direction, the other in completely opposite. Employees are not communicating in the way their boss is. Potential clients don't even remember the name or where to look up your business online. The social media posts are abruptly posted as if it's a personal account.

All this and many more hurdles occur when the preliminary steps are not followed. Brand assets should be guided by your brand strategy and never vice versa.

Begin With Brand Identifiers

The day you were born, you looked like any other child in the entire world. So, how did your parents identify you? They gave you a name. It was probably decided before your birth or after. What happened next as you grew up? You were given clothes of a particular style. You had a peculiar hair style.

You see where I'm going with this reference? People identified you with these visual characteristics which separate you from the rest of 8 billion people on earth.

This applies to a brand also in a similar manner. Your brand's first and foremost asset is your brand's name and logo. It's a visual cue for your audience to relate to a brand even when you're not there to present it.

Your Brand's Name And Logo

Every business owner has a brand logo these days but not everyone has it impactful with a story behind. Brand logos are not your brand definers because most of the time your logo will not introduce your brand.

Imagine looking at the instagram logo for the first time or the Facebook logo for the first time. Did you make out that the 'F' on

Facebook meant it was a social media platform? I guess not.

So, if they don't introduce your brand to the target audience, why put so much effort into getting the perfect one? Well, first of all, it need not be perfect and honestly it need not be permanent. Apple's logo used to be a bitten Apple with a rainbow overlay, remember?

Secondly, it's important to get the most appropriate one because a logo is what your audience will recognise the next time they'll want your services. It'll create a sense of belonging to a tribe, and a sense of genuine promise of quality to your clients. Moreover it'll be engraved in their memories for any future associations. Tell me, if I say the word, Audi or Nike, your mind automatically creates an image, doesn't it? That's the intangible power of your brand's logo.

I shall be detailing out the process of getting the right logo in one of my upcoming posts with case studies and introduction to the various types of logo designs.

Your Brand's Colour Palette

Colours have the power to impact our deepest feelings for what we're looking at. If you have ever Googled colour psychology, you'd find tons of emotions associated with each and every colour.

Now these emotions can vary from place to place based on the general notions or ethnicities or cultural associations. For the western world, black clothes are worn at a funeral while in India, it is white cloth. Red is often associated with a sign of danger but can also be a sign of energy and vigour. Similarly most of the colours are in a way linked with an emotional response from the general audience.

After understanding your brand qualities through the activities of brand strategy, you must have got a hint of what emotional qualities your brand offers.

Now, we need to set up a colour palette for your brand based on these qualities. These colours will ultimately be reflected in all your marketing activities, branding collaterals such as business cards, website, and many more.

Generally, a minimum of two and a maximum of five colours are to be decided upon with a neutral base of black, white or gray and a dominant colour. The dominant colour will also be reflected in your brand's logo if suitable. The colour wheel or some colour palette online resources are perfect for this task.

Make sure not to select plenty of primary or secondary colours as it will ultimately distract the audience from your main message. As an example, if colours red and yellow are used in your colour palette without any intended reason or balance, it can distract your audience from a singular message.

It's very important to keep it as minimal as possible in the current era. It's no longer the Art Nouveau or Renaissance eras where every colour has to be used unless of course that's what your brand is all about.

If uncertain, go for a single primary or secondary colour that suits your brand strategy and mix it up with neutral colours of black, white and gray. This is one of the most sophisticated colour palettes for decent brands. But make sure this colour palette is followed not excessively but genuinely in all your communications.

Your Brand's Typography/Typeface/Fonts

Fonts or typefaces or typography, an art of written

expression, is often neglected when communicating your brand to your clients. People think of fonts as the fancy decorative styles used by artists to portray art or craft. But, in fact, fonts have the ability to make or break your brand's image in the market.

Fonts have their own personality. Just like your brand, a font has the ability to evoke an emotional response. While some fonts are preferred for their clarity and universal readability, others are appreciated for their bold display or script like qualities.

Basically, your brand needs a base or global font which needs to identify your brand. Now, in general fonts are paired up in groups of two or three based on their usage in titles, headings and paragraphs. This pairing needs to compliment each other and your brand's identity.

If your brand is about sophisticated business, you cannot afford to have a fancy script font on your website's homepage. Also, if your brand's about fancy clothing designs, you cannot bore your clients with simple Times New Roman. Although it's safe to select a widely readable font, one should not hesitate to go for non conventional fonts or even get your own customised one.

Your Brand's Tone Of Voice Or Messages Or Communication Style

Each one of us has a particular style of communication whether it is written or spoken. Moreover, this style varies on the basis of where and with whom we communicate. It can be a sophisticated communication with our business partners or clients or a friendly and casual one with our peers.

Like movies or films, our brand's need to perform in the market. Some of them can perform with a wicked tone, while some can be comical. It can be straightforward, fancy, imaginative, thrilling, provocative, educational, business oriented, creative, boring, dramatic, cheesy, or whatever else you can think of.

What really matters in brand communications is the consistency and coherence in the tone and style of your messages! You cannot deliver your brand's message in a sophisticated manner on one platform and in a casual manner in the other. It loses its credibility in this manner.

This effort seems practically simpler to achieve through one person but is difficult to maintain throughout the team because each of us has a different communication style.

Your Brand's Use Of Imagery

The modern world literally runs on visuals and images. They are the elements which stay for long in the memories of our audience. The world is attracted towards good visuals, no matter how unfortunate or unfair it may sound . Now, your brand may or may not be producing the best visuals in the world but your branding should do so.

For example, if you're an interior designer, your visuals ought to be attractive. But if you're an engineering services designer, your HVAC layouts may not be the most beautiful ones. But, hey, who stops you from creating beautiful visuals that market your knowledge to the public? You must have seen the advertisements of smartphones these days and how they lure the public with the internal engineering of their devices. That's beauty.

Your brand's visuals can be your own graphics or photographs of your work or it can imagery related to your content bought from the internet. Anyway, it should have a consistent meaning. They will be displayed on your website and will act as a catalyst to your brand.

Now that you've learnt a thing or two about the various brand identifiers. It's time to use these tools to enhance your brand's identity.

Brand Touchpoints

Where and how should I use the brand assets?

> *A brand for a company is like a reputation for a person.*
> *You earn reputation by trying to do hard things well.*
>
> — JEFF BEZOS

You might be wondering, what to do with all the stuff that we created above? How to make use of that stuff to actually produce results for your service or product? Well, here comes the touchpoints or the virtual places where people will come across your brand.

Back in the old days, when the digital world wasn't the hype, people focused branding and marketing only to hoardings on billboards, handout newsletter prints, advertisements in newspapers, magazines, calling out people, yellow pages and what not.

This was not only exclusive to the rich and elite personalities but also too complex a process without any guarantee of results.

Today, when most of us own a digital device, we spend almost 70% of our time in a day on digital media. So, it seems only logical that we grab the attention of our audience from the digital media.

Also, since the uprising of this monstrous pandemic of COVID-19, everyone has suddenly shifted their social activities to some or the other kind of digital media platform.

So, without any further convincing, let's begin with developing your brand's touchpoints.

Your Brand's Website

I've already talked about the significance of a website in the modern times when almost everyone is living half of their lives on the internet.

Your website is the first and foremost touchpoint your clients or audience is going to look for!

Don't think of your website as your portfolio to simply show off your projects or skills. Think of it as your only means to communicate with a potential client, audience, student or someone who's simply curious about something you do.

Now, there are many websites available out there which can guide you to create your own website without much hassle or coding knowledge. My personal favourite is websitelearners.com.

But the real challenge lies in crafting that perfect website which conveys your brand's identity to the desired audience.

For beginners, getting the right message across in a minimal design is better than getting a heavy dynamic website design with fancy elements which often distract the viewers from your content.

Remember, your brand's website is not there to fix your broken business or service. Don't spend too much time and effort in decorating your website with fancy widgets and useless or forced content. This might create a sore experience for your viewers and they might never come back to visit.

Also, all the extra stuff often slows down a website, which in the modern days is worse than anything. Just look at the homepage of Google if you ever feel the need to fill your website!

Make A Content Strategy

Begin with a content strategy for your website. Instead of straightforward jumping into building the website, spend some time to create a mind map of how your website should look and feel, the kind of information it will display.

Apply The Brand Identifiers

Paint your website with the brand identifiers we developed in the last stage. Don't forget about your brand's style. Make sure your website has the typography, colours, logo, language and imagery which you decided earlier.

It's easy to be flattered by the availability of millions of options but stick to what you decided best for your brand earlier, or else you'll lose consistency in your brand's communication.

Less Is More

Keep it simple silly. Reduce the number of pages. People don't have the patience to flip through 10 pages to know what your work is all about.

Don't beat around the bush. If everything can be summarised in one or two pages, that's perfect.

Get A Blog And Keep It Updated

Don't forget about the Blog. You might be wondering, but I'm a business, not a blogger! Well, imagine there's a parent out there who wishes to renovate his house to cater to his child's growing needs.

So, he's got a challenge which he has never dealt with before. Like everyone else, he would go over the internet to look for a way he can do this on his own with minimal expenses.

Now, imagine he stumbles across your insightful blog post on your website regarding renovating houses for increasing family needs. He reads your blog post, feels that he understands what needs to be done and probably realises that he needs your help.

So, he contacts you and asks for consultancy services. You offer your great services, he refers you to his friends and ultimately you get more work. He's happy, you're more than happy. Everybody wins.

Now, do you realize the significance of that silly blog post which you were too lazy to write? This is the power of knowledge sharing these days. People don't trust you until you offer them knowledge first.

You can either get a content writer on board to write for your website's Blog but honestly you'll have to guide him or her in the direction towards meaningful content. Or else he or she will write fluff content which might be simply bulk nonsense words for your website that might fly away your viewers and potential clients.

Design The Website With Empathy Towards Viewer

Instead of making it about you, make the website for your viewers. Add content that guides a viewer to specific information such as your expertise, services, types of projects, statistics, testimonials, philosophy, journey, process, deliverables, etc. Let the viewer feel as if she has entered the perfect zone to sort her problems.

Too often designers make their websites too abstract and artsy as if your website is like an art gallery.

A particular page can be, there's nothing wrong with it. But please expose yourself to the viewer. Make it easy for her to reach you out. Let it have human like qualities. Let your website do the conversation while you sleep in one time zone.

Quality Over Quantity On Website.

Are you worried that you don't have much to show on the website? Probably, you must've done just one project. Quantity doesn't matter in branding and marketing. In fact, companies, designers, or businesses which tend to focus on quantity rather than quality often confuses their audience ultimately bringing down overall sales.

In today's competitive world, it's best to be as specific and minimal as possible. You might stand out from all the noise.

Now, even if you have one project or service or product, you need to find a way to portray the maximum linkages associated with it.

For example, you've got one interior design project. So, you talk about the journey behind that project, the materials, the design, the statistics, the outcomes and learnings, it's future benefits, how it makes the clients feel, and so much more.

Now, take for example you've designed a logo in your entire design career to now. Show the iterations behind it, the combinations, the grids, it's message, it's derivation, it's meaning for the company, it's perception to the general public, it's adaptation to various media, and a lot more.

Both these examples are what I can recall from my own experience and honestly, you show me your work and I can give you a hundred things to talk about what you did. But that's my strength.

You need to portray your brand's strength in a similar manner on your website no matter if you've just done one project, made one product that you feel will change the world or one service that you feel will help humanity or one business that you think will make our lives easier in the tough times.

Don't Overdo. Don't Overthink. Don't Over-Spend.

Last point which I must stress over anything else is don't overthink your brand's website because you'll never get it perfect. It can be changed always but that doesn't mean you divert all your focus from your main business to designing the website. Remember that it's a brilliant catalyst for your brand but at some point you need to get it over with and get back to your brilliant work.

Like any other design, this task of getting the perfect website for your brand can be full of anxiety and indecisiveness. But remember, you need to set a deadline and put it out there in perpetual motion to spread your brand's awareness as soon as possible.

Or else you'll spend months getting the perfect website which you could've devoted to marketing your brand and business. So, just take a decision and so being so indecisive as your website is not your business, it's a catalyst!

Brand Logo

7 secret rules you never knew for a successful brand logo

> "A brand is no longer what we tell the consumer it is
> —it is what consumers tell each other it is."
>
> SCOTT COOK

There are a million brand logos out there in the world. There might be even more logos available than brands out there. But what makes a logo stand out from the noise.

Good logos follow certain rules which experienced graphic designers stumble upon after years of hit and trials. Clients might be genius with their designs but a few know how a logo works. So, it's better to give them a helping hand.

Here are the 7 secret rules you never knew for a successful brand logo:

Good Logos Simply Identify. They Don't Describe Or Elaborate A Brand.

A good logo tells the audience what a brand is but not what it does. It's like your friend's name. He might be called by Jane or John but it doesn't tell you whether he's a nice man or a jerk.

Most clients want a logo that shows what they do or what product or service they sell.

Now, imagine if Apple Computers Inc. had a macintosh as their first logo instead of half bitten apple, they would have to change their branding when they invented the iPod and the iPhone. Whereas remaining neutral and focusing on an abstract and clear identifier, clients can evolve and grow in any direction.

A Good Logo Can't Solve All Your Business Problems.

A brand's logo is only meant to reinforce your brand's message. It cannot improve your service or product or your shipping hurdles. It's like a good armani suit which makes you look good in a party but it cannot possibly help you change your foul mouth personality.

A Good Logo Should Be Visually Engaging.

A logo should be visually clear and strong. It should be seen from across the room. Often weak, quiet and recessive logos disappear in the long run and the modern day noise. Tiny lines, itsy-bitsy typography, pastel colours rarely succeed against bold elements in a brand's logo.

A Good Logo Must Have Mnemonic Value.

In short, it should be memorable. One of the best tools to adopt is to pose a question such as 'Why is the letter O in this logo red in color?' or 'What's this arrow in FedEx supposed to mean?' or 'What is meant by the smile swoosh in the Amazon logo?'.

The time spent by the audience pondering over such questions makes a particular logo highly memorable.

A Good Logo Must Be Able To Exist In A Variety Of Media.

20 years ago, most of the brand logos existed on the print media. Today they need to be designed for the digital world such as for websites, mobile apps, social media platforms, etc. You need to make sure the brand logo is highly adaptable to the various media and doesn't get pixelated or seems invisible on some mobile apps.

A Logo Is Not An Illustration.

An illustration is an illustration. A brand logo is not an illustration, it's not a piece of complex art. It should not be complicated to reproduce.

A Logo Is The Foundation Of The Visual System.

A logo is the entry point to a brand's message. Although the entire identity system is the whole story, no logo should be out of context from the rest of brand identifiers.

Also, always test a brand logo on an app or a website or some platform to understand how it behaves in the context. A fabulous looking logo on your 15" screen might not be readable on your mobile screen.

That's all for the rules one must follow for a successful brand logo. You might not remember these for the rest of your life but it's a good practice to take a step back and evaluate your brand's logo based on the above rules once in a while.

∞∞∞

Create a brand logo

What everyone must know about a brand logo?

"Design is the silent ambassador of your brand."

PAUL RAND

Today, there are many words to describe a brand logo. One might call it a wordmark, an icon, a symbol, signature, ID, Brandmark, Trademark, etc. While we can't track all the ways to call a logo, we will stick to the good old basics to understand how a brand's logo is ultimately designed.

In the following 4 chapters we will talk about wordmark, monogram, icon, logo; their upside and downside; and how they can help reinforce a brand's identity in their own unique way.

We will also learn how to decide which kind of arrangement suits best to your brand's message but that's for the next set of chapters where we will learn the step-by-step process of getting an impactful brand logo for yourself or your client.

Brand Logo

When someone tries to understand what he or she means by the word logo, it gets tricky. For some, it is only the icon, Wordmark, or monogram. For some, it is the brand, which is purely wrong.

A logo is a wordmark, monogram, icon or a combination of a wordmark and icon or monogram and icon.

It is the final form that your audience should see. A combination of wordmark and icon reinforces the connection and increases recognition in the market.

For example, the target logo has a red icon and all letterforms in caps.

A logo is the formal wear of the brand identity system.

As an example, the NBS logo has letters designed to match the visual language of the peacock icon.

Similarly, in the brand logo of Baskin robbins, the letters

combine to form an interesting number which depicts the total flavors owned by the company. This might be a coincidence but it is surely engaging for a brand's audience.

But combining a wordmark and icon by dropping a symbol on top of the wordmark or next to it is not the only solution. It is half the job done. Merging the two in a unique and creative manner creates an easy way to use the logo that can't be separated into two distinguishable parts.

The main point of understanding the terminology of logos is not to create a complex language. There are so many misunderstood terminologies, that when getting your brand logo right, you and your audience should be talking about the same thing.

Wordmark

Here's how your company's name can be your brand's logo.

"A brand's strength is built upon its determination to promote its own distinctive values and mission."

JEAN-NOEL KAPFERER

In short, a wordmark is a company's name as a logo. It sounds simple and is one of the most widely used options for a logo worldwide. In brief, it is a company's name with a customized typeset in a proprietary way and used consistently across all brand communication. It has been a pretty successful option since history such as Ford, Facebook, Google, Knoll, etc.

So what are the upsides to this? First of all, it is easy to identify. It is easy to read and know who and what the company is. There is no need to decipher or remember any complex icon or symbol. But there are some downsides to this simplicity. It heavily relies on reading. It may not be easily comprehensible in other languages across the world. Some companies such as Coca Cola transcend this problem but it took almost 100 years and billions of dollars to be recognised globally by the cursive shape of its letterforms and the proprietary glass bottle design.

Another downside is that people tend to make such logos on their own by copying it in a disproportionate manner. So, it should be unique to discourage people from copying it. For this, it should be a customised proprietary typeset instead of out of the box font, which should be easy to read and memorable.

A wordmark is an icon of a brand name. They are letterforms modified to read faster and in a simplified form.

This is never possible with out of the box fonts available on the internet. While getting a customized or transformed typeface for your brand logo, don't fixate on sans-serif fonts as they look sophisticated or professional.

Feel free to opt for a script font with fancy characters if your business or service is such. Imagine if the Coca Cola logo was a sans-serif wordmark, would we associate it with something that we enjoy at parties? Strive towards creating an iconic representation of the name that expresses the brand attributes.

We have discussed brand attributes in our previous posts and I would like you to keep going back and forth to remind yourself what your company does the best. It's easy to deviate from your brand message and choose a wordmark that seems wonderful in isolation but doesn't really communicate your brand message.

Monogram

How can a monogram be your brand's logo?

> "Too many companies want their brands to reflect some idealized, perfected image of themselves. As a consequence, their brands acquire no texture, no character, and no public trust."
>
> — RICHARD BRANSON

When we hear the word monogram, we usually think about initials on a T-shirt or a handkerchief. It is also a widely used term in Branding and Marketing.

A monogram is, in short, a company's initials or combined initials to create a logo.

It is a pretty good solution if the company brand has a long or complicated name. People tend to remember short and crispy names but it is possible if by chance a company has evolved over the years and has a name that not only is long in writing but also difficult to pronounce due to certain linguistic anomaly.

Making a monogram also helps a brand to move into new territories and ventures by eliminating a name that may no longer apply.

As an example, IBM which was originally International Business Machines moved away from a logo that displayed its full name. This helped IBM to move into other businesses with ease.

Similarly, the NASA logo by Richard Dan transformed National Aeronautics and Space Administration which was a mouthful to a monogram that was easy to remember. Similar was the case with MTV from music television, American Broadcasting company to ABC, and many more.

The downside to a monogram is the ubiquity of acronyms in the world. There are so many sets of initials out there that one can be confused easily. Like, UBS, is it a bank or a TV Channel. Like, NASA, is it the space organization or the National Association of Students of Architecture in India. There is a possibility of confusion and misunderstanding.

Although, the upside to a monogram is the faster recognition. There's an ability to create a brand with more options than a descriptive name much like what IBM did. Oftentimes it is suggested to use the monogram with a descriptive Wordmark attached to it for a sufficient amount of time until the audience relates and remembers the monogram.

∞∞∞

Icon

When to use an icon as your brand logo?

> "Your premium brand had better be delivering something special, or it's not going to get the business."
>
> WARREN BUFFET

Our lives are filled with all kinds of symbols. We are easily informed of simple signs such as cross and plus without any guidance. Also, we are pretty much aware of complex symbols such as country flags which communicate patriotism or an apple that communicates knowledge.

An icon is a symbol used as a logo. It heavily relies on symbolism.

It only works when we understand what they actually mean and whom they belong to. They are incredibly powerful in crossing cultural boundaries and languages.

But the problem is that there are too many icons today that it takes a long time for one to become successful and recognisable.

An icon can be a straightforward literal symbol like that of greyhound or puma. Or it can be an abstract composition like Nike's swoosh or three stripes of Adidas.

Icons that have succeeded took years of repeated exposure before they could stand on their own in the market.

The half bitten apple logo of Apple Inc. had its name attached to its bottom for nearly 2 decades before dropping the name.

Icon is not an illustration. It is not a complex piece of art. It is a symbol reproduced in all media communicating your brand's message. For example, the Chaseman Hat was based on a chinese coin, the CBS eye icon and many more.

Overly abstract icons are hard to remember. For several years, many business clients wanted to convey the same message of 'coming together'. The result was that lots of icons emerged with strange shapes merging in the center. This may have communicated the general idea abstractly but they were so ubiquitous that the audience did not see them. It simply failed.

When the solution to a brand's logo is an icon, I suggest that we link the name to the symbol for at least a few years. This gives the audience time to recognise it. It may seem like hammering them with the same idea over and over again. But you and your client see the icon all day long but the audience will see it just for a second.

Branding is about communicating the message. It takes time and typically repeated exposure.

It's an old saying,"Tell the audience what information you're going to tell them, then tell them that information, then tell them what you just told them".

∞∞∞

Wordmark as a brand logo.

12 steps to create a successful wordmark.

Before deciding on whether to get an icon, wordmark, or monogram, it is advisable to revisit your brand attributes.

Don't thrash around trying anything expecting the perfect solution to simply pop up magically out of the blue without no order. We obviously need to explore the variations of each type i.e. wordmark, monogram, and icon in order to reach at a conclusion with a brand logo that conveys your brand's logo in the most apt manner.

Start with the wordmark. At some point, I need to see the brand name with or without the icon. Soon you'll realize that letterforms work together in surprising ways to create interesting forms that can support your brand's message.

Follow these steps!

For this we will follow the step by step process:

1. Set up a blank page in adobe illustrator or Corel draw whatever you feel comfortable. I would suggest illustrator as it offers a variety of options to customize the typeset.

2. Set up a landscape layout of 11" by 17". This size is majorly used by graphic designers for logo designs iterations.

3. Next, type in the brand name in any random font on the left extreme corner.

4. Repeat this on 4 rows across and 4 rows down in a variety of favorable fonts. You can download the fonts from https://fonts.google.com/. There are many free source websites for fonts but Google fonts offer us the ability to view a brand name in a variety of trending fonts in real-time.

5. Work your way down each font and observe each of them closely. Don't stop and edit any of them just yet. Just get yourselves a feel of the fonts.

6. Keep going and fill up a couple of more pages with at least 32 variations of favorable fonts.

7. Duplicate all these and change the case to lowercase. Now you have 64 typographical variations of your brand name.

8. Choose your favourite 8 options as 2 from each page. 4 from uppercase and 4 from lowercase.

9. Next, play with the arrangement of the typeset. Try stacked, horizontally aligned, change scale of one word, find interesting interlocking shapes.

10. From these options, select your favourite 3 options.

11. Since, the typeset which is a standard font is not your proprietary, go and refine the letterforms.

12. Work with each version, until you reach one that is strong and matches your brand's attributes.

Conclusion

This is no longer a word. It's an icon of a word. Congratulations, you've made your first wordmark. This is the first step in getting your brand's logo.

You don't need to refine it to death now. At this stage, you're in a draft stage, get some reviews from your peers or show it to your clients and then move on to refinement.

But before fixating on the wordmark, we will try the options of a monogram and an icon, because you never know a brilliant logo might just come out from your further experiments. So, don't just stop now.

Monogram as a brand logo.

`9 steps to create a successful Monogram.`

Even if you feel there's no need for a monogram, you need to explore the options. You never know you might stumble upon something wonderful.

Although pretty much most of the steps we will follow in creating a monogram will be similar to that of a wordmark, you need to understand that creating a monogram is a complex task yet a creative one as we'll be playing with individual letterforms.

Follow these steps!

So let's begin with the steps:

1. Set up a blank page in adobe illustrator or corel draw whatever you feel comfortable. I would suggest illustrator as it offers a

variety of options to customise the typeset.

2. Set up a landscape layout of 11" by 17". This size is majorly used by graphic designers for logo designs iterations.

3. Next, type in the brand name initials in any random font on the left extreme corner.

4. Repeat this on 4 rows across and 4 rows down in a variety of favorable fonts. You can download the fonts from https://fonts.google.com/. There are many free source websites for fonts but Google fonts offer us the ability to view a brand name in a variety of trending fonts in real-time.

5. Work your way down each font and observe each of them closely. Don't stop and edit any of them just yet. Just get yourselves a feel of the fonts.

6. Keep going and fill up a couple of more pages with at least 32 variations of favorable fonts.

7. Duplicate all these and change the case to lowercase. Now you have 64 typographical variations of your brand name.

8. Choose your favourite 8 options as 2 from each page. 4 from uppercase and 4 from lowercase.

9. Next, play with the arrangement of the typeset. Do they make interesting negative forms when they are connected? Is it easier to read the uppercase or lowercase? Are there similar shapes in the letter that can be made consistent such as circles or lines?

Conclusion

Don't torture the letters. Worst monogram logos are the ones that look painful. If the letters don't naturally lend themselves to the modification, don't force it

Monograms are tough to make but not impossible. And resolving all the complexity often leads to some of the most successful logos of all times. You need to discover a unique element in the logo. And most importantly, the solution must contribute to the brand's attribute.

Next, we will explore the creation of icons as a brand's logo.

∞∞∞

Icon as a brand logo.

8 steps to create a successful icon.

Till now we have played around with creating brand wordmarks and monograms. Now we shall explore the step by step guide to creating a compelling yet subtle icon for a brand's logo.

Overuse is one of the biggest issues with icons. Since businesses tend to emulate other businesses that have succeeded in the past. There's a repetition in brand strategy and mission.

From a local corner bistro in the countryside to a fortune 500 company, everyone wants to communicate the same messages of growth, global thinking, innovation, community and quality.

These jargons lead to logos that are indistinguishable and

give rise to too many radially emerging circular forms.

Audience responds better when the icon is represented by an easily distinguishable symbol connected to the brand message.

Follow these steps!

Moving on, let's have a look at the steps to create an impactful icon:

1. When starting with an icon, start with words known as guiding attributes. For example, creativity, respect, affordable, honest, green, innovative. Now obviously you need to follow your brand's guiding attributes.

2. Brainstorm concepts that serve as symbols for each guiding attribute. For example, creativity can be portrayed by a palette, key, paintbrush, lightbulb, crayon, nest or something else.

3. Now explore different ways to express these symbols visually. Sketch or draw digitally by referencing images

4. Don't worry about refining these too much just yet. Get a quick sketch idea.

5. Once exhausted all options, choose 3 of your favourite and refine them.

6. Stay with a black and white option. Don't be swayed by colours just yet. If it's not convincing in black and white, just dispose it off and start off with new options.

7. Once you start refining, go back to brand attributes and apply colour based on your brand's message. You don't want a cheerful pancake brand to be all gray and a computer business to be painted pink.

8. Don't stick to one option. If it looks ugly, move on. You can always go back and see something you missed.

Conclusion

By the end, you should have 3-4 possible symbols drawn in a style that reflects your brand.
Now it's time to put it all back together to create your brand's final logo.

10 steps to create a successful brand logo.

By now, our journey in the study and creation of wordmark, monogram and icon is complete. And I must congratulate you if you've made it this far.

Now let's reveal the final stepping stone of determining a complete logo.

Most designers take the icon and stick it next to the wordmark. It's half the job and it sucks.

The goal is to have a unified logo that is harmonious and connected in terms of shape, scale and position. It takes some exploring to reach the best solution.

Without wasting any more time, let's get on with our steps to compiling a brand logo:

Follow these steps!

1. Start by using the same 11" x 17" landscape layout in adobe illustrator or corel draw.

2. Take your 3-4 favorite icons which you developed in the previous articles.

3. Add your favorite wordmarks and monogram choices beside it in separate pages or artboards.

4. Now it's time to mix and match. I know it doesn't sound particularly analytical. But we need to slowly funnel your options to a tighter selection.

5. Combine each wordmark with each icon.

6. Combine each monogram with each icon.

7. Finally combine each monogram with a wordmark.

8. Some of these might be horrible. Some of these might be great. You need to go through each permutation combination in order to get that perfect match. But just don't fixate on one yet.

9. Choose 3 of your favourite from the above options.

10. On each logo, create a grid to unify the forms. Play around with proportions of icon and wordmark. Doing this makes the forms related and not arbitrary.

Final version of this is the lock-up. If they are separated, the brand's message will be weakened. This is the way they will be always communicated. This is a single unit and a piece of art that isn't adjustable by others using the logo.

It sounds pretty tight and an anxious activity. But you've taken the abstract concepts of your brand's messages into a physical and visual form. That deserves respect and appreciation.

Conclusion

That's it for the journey of creating a brand logo. I hope it was pretty exhaustive and exciting. I know merely reading these articles will do you no good but surely the knowledge fed into your subconscious mind will help you out in creating your brand logo or even selecting one with a graphic designer.

∞∞∞

Blogging for Designers

Why blogging is necessary for your design career?

> "Brands should think of themselves not as storytellers but storybuilders. We plant seeds of content and let our community build on it."
>
> — AMY PASCAL

A picture speaks a thousand words. Well, if you're a designer or know one, you'll know what I'm talking about. But today I'm here to tell you that blogging about design in very few words can boost your design career to great heights. Blogging is not something new. It's as old as the internet and today it is the ultimate tool that offers everyone the right to information and knowledge sharing.

Do you remember the days when one had to buy an expensive recipe book only to be dissapointed by the unavailibility of *ingredients? Or when we had those humongous encyclopedia books that would burn a hole in our pockets?*

Well, those were the days when information wasn't a fingerprint lock away! But today we are living in the age of digital information and never before has the right to share knowledge been so convenient! This is where blogging arrives as the perfect tool to boost your design career.

You might be wondering that being a designer you aren't passionate about writing or exploding your designs. You know you designs are pretty self explanatory and have served your clients pretty well in the past.

Well, let me take off that blindfold of your eyes and give you a few reasons why blogging is necessary for your design career!

Design Doesn't Speak For Itself.

As said above, a good visual might attract someone for a short period of time but it will not tell the story behind your designs. Your designs might be perfectly composed with the perfect color pallette and might offer the perfect user experience for your app users.

But who's going to tell the world about it? You blog will! This is the most important reason why you need a blog today!

Now you might be wondering that design is an iterative and highly complex process. What can one possibly write about a couple of sketches and visuals?

Well, there's a story behind every great design. So, if you feel your design is not a careless mistake then I'm here to tell you exactly how to craft the perfect story for your design blog.

You need to begin with the context, the clients, the requirements, the story behind how you got the project and how you percieved it. Then move ahead with the initial concepts or ideas and try to remember what were the motivating factors behind that first sketch. Then probably go on with the journey behind the design process, your inspirations, the conversations and so on.

You're Not Always There To Explain Your Design.

This is a no brainer. It's common sense. During client meetings, you're there to explain your designs but are you there for the people looking to hire an awesome designer over the internet?

Remember the amount of effort you had put into speaking about your design the last time you sat with your clients. Do you remember how many times you had to say the same thing?

Now imagine if you put the same amount of effort once to craft an informative and interesting blog article about a particular topic. Let's say the topic is your design process and how it helps clients maximise their business potential.

Do you realise how comfortable and engaging it will be for your prospective clients and yourself to let them read a blog article rather than you blabbering for hours?!

That's the power of blogging! It can be your alter ego to help grow your design career in all the time zones even while you are dozing off.

Design Has A Weird Language.

Let's all agree to this statement. A wall texture isn't suddenly poetic and solves all my family issues! We, designers, need to realize this sooner or later that our perception is way different and complex than the normal world. And so is our language.

I'll give you a pretty good example behind this. During my years at architecture college I read a lot of books on architecture theory and philosophies which made me realize how distinct and desolated our language is from the layman.

This barrier needs to be broken for designers to be recognized outside their shells! If your design helps your user with a smooth and simplified user experience then why can't your language be comprehensible to the masses?

I've visited tons of design websites and digital portfolios which talk about the artistic beauty or the poetic value of their designs. The next time you blog about your design, talk about how it offers great value to your clients, or how a particular color choice triggers certain emotions, or about the use of sustainable materials in your interiors!

Talk about the stuff that 'really' matters to the clients and end users of your designs!

Designers Get Recognition Through Good Stories.

You must have heard about the best designers around the world in a field of your interest.

Who is it? Where did you learn about their work? Did you watch their documentary? Was it a particular show on Netflix? Do you get recommendations about their work in your email or on google news? Do you admire their style?

Great designs are like great fairy tales. It's almost impossible to believe them to be true. *There's this quote, " Form follows fiction'.*

At any point while you watch the documentary of your favorite designer, do you get that desire to be recognized? Your blog can be the first milestone towards recognition. It can offer people an insight into your design philosophy, design processes, delivery methods, struggles, mistakes, learnings, and realization of the project.

So, the next time you sit down to write a blog post for your design, think about crafting a good story. Don't worry if you don't know how because I'll be sharing a couple of actionable tips for this in the coming articles!

Clients Prefer Designers With Thoughts At Similar Frequency.

You must have felt this when in a conversation with your clients. There are certain people who vibe with your philosophies and beliefs.

Imagine you're in a conversation with a client from the healthcare industry. She believes that her company creates products which offer people nutrition and better health through herbal solutions. She believes in values of sustainability, organic cure, natural treatment and a holistic well being. Now let's say she approaches you for an interior design of her new workspace for her employees. She goes online and comes across your blog post on *'The benefits of indoor plants for a workspace'*. Voila! She's interested in your design sense and wants you to design her workspace!

That's how ideas resonate at similar frequencies amongst people with similar mindsets. That's how your blog can attract potential clients!

Conclusion

Well how did you like the 5 great reasons why blogging is necessary for your design career? There are a few more reasons like blogging can boost your digital presence, a design blog can inspire younger generations, it can supplement your portfolio if works and ultimately it can perform as an archive of your journey as a designer. I hope I was able to convince some of you to get started on with your design blog!

Bonus: 101 Blog Ideas

Blogging for Architects & Interior Designers

"Your brand is a story unfolding across all customer touch points."

JONAH SACHS

So, you've got your website up and running with an empty blog section on it. Are you wondering what to write on it? Well, here I am going to give out more than a 100 blog ideas for architects and interior designers to write on!

Yes, you heard it right! A 101 blog ideas to write on! What are you waiting for?

Often architects and interior designers communicate their designs in a language that is comprehensible to their own community and no one else.

Here the blog ideas are carefully crafted to help your architecture or interior design website to attract more clients and customers.

Empathy is the key. When I sat down to write this blog post, I sat in the shoes of an anonymous client or customer looking for the services of a great architect or interior designers. Now, unlike what architects and interior designers think of their designs, laymen clients think about a whole different world.

Clients are concerned about the value a particular design will offer them rather than the wallpaper being too poetic. Their priority is functionality rather than aesthetics. Some might argue that aesthetics are sufficient to lure or seduce a client by showing beautiful renderings. Anyways, that's not the case.

So, writing about the topics that concern your clients will certainly help you gain more authenticity, they'll start understanding the process and efforts behind your designs and ultimately will offer you an opportunity to ask for a fair payment for your time and effort.

Without further beating around the brush following are the blog ideas I would suggest architects and interior designers to consider writing on for their blogs!

1. Why one must hire an architect or an interior designer?

2. What is the difference between good design and bad design?

3. What are the factors that guide a good design?

4. What contemporary trends are followed in design?

5. In what ways can a designer add business value to a space?

6. How do architects and interior designers work?

7. What goes into coming up with great design solutions?

8. How to arrange furniture to optimise space usage and movement?

9. How modern technology can assist in communicating designs?

10. How particular materials can offer great value to a space?

11. Why is it necessary to invest in good quality interior fixtures?

12. How good design or bad design can impact the experience of users in a space?

13. Why is it necessary for architecture to allow natural light inside a space?

14. How can architecture and interior design impact your health and well being?

15. What kind of plants to choose for interior and why?

16. What is sustainable architecture and how does it impact business?

17. What qualities to look for in the architecture and interior design firm you hire?

18. What mistakes to avoid while hiring an architecture and interior design firm?

19. How to proceed on a contract with an architecture or interior design firm?

20. What scale or kind of architecture or interior design firm skills you approach?

21. How should you negotiate the terms and payment with an architecture and interior design firm?

22. Why must you never hesitate to way in your own opinion on an architecture or interior design?

23. What basics you must know before approaching an architect or interior designer for a project?

24. Why must you have patience for a good architecture and interior design to evolve?

25. How to understand basic architectural drawings for a project?

26. Why you must refrain from exploiting architects and interior designers?

27. Where to look for an architect or interior designer for your next project?

28. How can building automation optimize your expenditure on bills?

29. Pinterest or Google search cannot design the perfect space for your project.

30. Design is not for free. Designers have got bills to pay too.

32. What you must know about the design process of an

architect or interior designer?

33. You are heavily mistaken if you think architecture or interior design is not a worthy skill.

34. How can good architecture generate high revenue for a commerical project?

35. How can good interior design attract more customers to your showroom?

36. How can good architecture increase the sales of your real estate?

37. How can good interior design increase memberships of your gymnasium or wellness center?

38. Why must you refrain from copying architecture styles from greece temples.

39. Enough with out of context designs. Enough ornamentation in the post modern era.

40. How can appropriately designed office Interiors impact workplace culture?

41. Why your office workplace productivity is low because of bad architecture and interior design.

42. Impact of architecture and interior design on daily routine and ultimately lifestyle.

43. Power of good or bad design to impact the well being of patients in a hospital.

44. How natural landscape within a space can impact the

health and well being of its users?

45. How will architecture and interior design change in the coming future?

46. How is technology changing the way we use our spaces?

47. How to design compact yet efficient spaces within small areas?

48. Why should we negotiate with the quality of space when the space is less or expensive?

49. How to get returns on investment from your property through good architecture?

50. How to renovate and adaptively reuse your old property into revenue generating space?

51. How can particular colors impact the quality of space you're living in?

52. How to select the perfect colours for your interiors?

53. What goes into designing the perfect interiors for your project?

54. How to integrate a brand with good architecture and interior design?

55. Enhance brand identity through interior space branding.

56. How do architects and interior designers do a perfect job at interior space branding?

57. Why is it necessary for business owners to explain their brand to architects and interior designers before their project

begins.

58. What's the process behind a good architecture and interior design for clients to know.

59. What's the difference between an architect, architectural designer, interior designer, contractors, project manager and a civil engineer?

60. How to keep a track of the project with the architect or interior designer?

61. Why is it necessary to be clear of your goals and not the requirements before approaching an architect or interior designer?

62. Why is it necessary to give a certain level of freedom to your architect or interior designer while working on a project?

63. What kind of architecture or interior design studio to approach for your next project?

64. How the design of a particular project added value to the clients.

65. How certain design elements added value to a space.

66. Number of ways in which architects and interior designers can bring life to a dead space.

67. How to comprehend payement methods and schedules adopted by architects and interior designers.

68. How did the design of a particular project evolve from concepts to reality?

69. A day in the life of an architect or interior designer.

70. What do your clients say about your projects and your working culture?

71. Customer review of your previously completed projects.

72. Style of architecture in a particular region where you work in.

73. Tours and travels of the architect or interior designer to explore inspirations behind the work.

74. News and trends from architecture and design from around the world.

75. Opinions about certain architecture and interior design projects.

76. Critics and personal perspectives over latest developments in building industry.

77. Noteworthy architecture from around the world.

78. Inspiration lists or moodboards or collections of online or print content.

79. Stories and journeys of lives of architects and interior designers.

80. Content not related to design and how everyday life impacts design.

81. Emotions and values associated with design.

82. Share your personal philosophies regarding your practice or style.

83. Share your personal resources on templates, designs, elements, etc.

84. Interviews or discussions or casual conversations that give insight into design process.

85. Impact of different cultures on architecture and interior design.

86. Significance of visual design principles in architecture and interior design.

87. Talk about other stakeholders involved in a project.

88. Talk about collaboration in a project.

89. Talk about the various kinds of space designers like landscape designers, stage designers, graphic designers, artists, engineers, planners, etc.

90. Talk about current global challenges.

91. Talk about how architecture and interior design can help solve global challenges.

92. Talk about how best practices in design can help people lead a better life.

93. Talk about the problems in our current urban environments.

94. Talk about the significance of good space design on mental health.

95. Talk about the impact of good design of people of different age groups.

96. Talk about the link of space design with ethnography and anthropology.

97. Write about how good design can impact certain neglected sections of the society.

98. Write about current trends of community participation, social housing, organizing the informal sector, etc.

99. Write about transformations in best practices of architecture and design.

100. Write about the ways in which design needs to adapt to the future generations.

101. Write about the values associated with good architecture design much like a good UX.

Acknowledgement

The knowledge portrayed above in the book is an accumulation of years of experience and learning through brand experts, professional designers and a lot more. I've stood on the shoulders of giants.

Books By This Author

Visual Dialogues 101 Graphic Design Fundamentals: Design Career, Layout, Typography, And Colour

A picture really does speak 1000 words. 90% of information out there in the world transmitted to our brains is visual. Visual images are processed 60,000 times faster than long form text. 67% of business owners across the globe expect that visual design will be even more important to the success of their businesses over the next decade. The world around us is changing at an exponential pace. Our attention spans are reducing to micro-seconds day by day as we are fed content through innumerable sources around us from the television to our smartphones. Our lifestyles are inclined towards visual aesthetics more than ever before. We view the world more through our camera lenses than our other senses. Part of it is sad but most of it is revolutionary. Visual design has never been a more powerful tool offering us freedom and opportunity to inform, express, evoke, educate, promote and make our lives more interesting than ever before.

Graphic design has been around us since the inception of time. From symbols on walls, paintings in caves, carvings on artifacts to the modern-day packaging, posters, brochures, advertisements, social media, web layouts, app designs and a lot more, visual design has been true to its purpose of creative communication. We all are essentially storytellers. All of us have different stories to communicate to one another. At times we love to share our exciting stories by narrating them to our friends but often we wish to share these stories with the whole world in an attractive and emotive manner. Here, graphic design plays a significant role.

Graphic designers are people like you and me who have devoted their lives to the noble service of helping individuals and businesses to craft their stories to the world in the most expressive manners. It takes years of study and practice and failure and learnings to achieve a decent sense of graphic design and this is the reason why it is the most sought-after profession in the modern world of media and content. This book is an intensive guide to either begin your career in graphic design or to reinforce your existing graphic skills by offering you a window into the basics and advanced concepts behind numerous design decisions.

If you have no prior experience with graphic design but wish to taste the creative waters of this design career, this book is a perfect journey for you to take as soon as possible. You might be worried about graphic design being associated with artistic skills of painting, sketching or what not but let me assure you, a designer is not at all an artist. There's a mile long wall between the fields of art and design. Designers are problem solvers and artists are talented individuals who express their own style to the world. Designers work for the enhancement of their user's experience and to bridge the gap of communication. Art can be subjective but design cannot afford to be. So, don't worry if your artistic skills are not extraordinary, you can still be a visual designer.

How will this book benefit you? It's not at all like your everyday design college reference book. The book begins by covering topics ranging from design careers, benefits of sketching, media for presenting design, fundamentals of design, the creative brief and process, research and creating ideas, and production. Then it picks up each of the three pillars of graphic design i.e., layout, typography and colour and digs deep into the fundamental concepts, guidelines, mistakes and practical applications for a holistic understanding of design. A unique feature of this book are the 112 square graphics created to assist the written text within the paragraphs because you know, an image with text is 500% more impactful than plain rambling in text. You'll realize this fact when you'll finally become a successful visual designer after reading this book. Now let's begin the exciting journey to the wonderland of visual design!

Diary Of A Young Indian Architect: Space, Time And Life

This book is part fiction and part non-fiction. It's a collection of thoughts, tales, and insightful stories written over a span of five years during my college years at the School of Planning and Architecture, Bhopal, India.

It's a collection of diary entries, informative articles, essays, travel tales, fiction stories, poems, and contemplative articles on a wide variety of topics such as living in an Indian college, explorations in France, the condition of our metropolitan Indian cities, architecture storytelling, thoughts on modern-day lifestyle and a lot more!

Through this book, I would like to express my heartfelt gratitude to all my college mates, friends, seniors, teachers, and mentors for all the memorable moments, learnings, laughter, and all the life lessons.

Dear Me, Letters To My Younger Self

It's the year 2021 and we're all stuck inside our homes under our blankets. An insane pandemic hit the world in March 2020 with the spread of a highly contagious virus called coronavirus or Covid 19. It has transformed our lives like never before.

It was 2 a.m. in the night. It was just me alone with my night lamp, a cup of green tea, a fountain pen, my beloved black diary, and an antique typewriter gifted to me by my grandfather.

As I read the last words of his letter, the ink vanished into thin air leaving me baffled yet excited to get on with my mission. I kept my pen and paper aside and dragged the typewriter towards me. I closed my eyes and went into a short flashback of my entire life until now. My face went from smiles into sadness to grin to laughter to remorse as I remembered all the precious moments and regrets. My fingers grazed all over the alphabet keys while I kept my eyes closed and my emotions got the best of me. I took a deep breath and started typing the first letter to my younger self.

Imagine if you were allowed to send letters to your own past? What would you do? What would you love to change about your past that would impact your today?!

A Handloom Weaver's Village In Maheshwar: Architecture Design Thesis 2019 | Vernacular & Traditional Architecture | Housing | Village | India

A compilation of years of research, strategy and design in the form of an architecture design thesis. It explores the fields of vernacular architecture, Indian villages, textiles, weaver colonies in India, and ways in which people transform their homes into workspaces to accomodate heavy equipments of handloom weaving. The thesis is based on a small but prominent weaver's village in Maheshwar located in the heart of central India i.e. Madhya Pradesh. The village is famous for its revival of the handloom culture and its institutional environment to preserve the rich traditional knowledge systems of handloom weaving over mechanised powerloom weaving. This thesis dives deep into the roots of humans and their associations with their spaces majorly their houses.

It's a good reference guide for young architecture students looking for a case study or for researchers to understand the true spirit of Indian architecture which doesn't lie in the barren monuments but the our own villages where people craft their own spaces in the kost sustainable manner possible!

Building Your Brand Assets: Brand Name, Story, Color, Typography, Tone Of Voice, Imagery, Illustrations, Iconography, Style Guide

Your brand is and should be unique. It should stand out from others in a similar business or service. What makes your brand so different? It's your unique promise and value that you provide to your customers and clients. But how do you communicate this to your potential network? Through branding.

Like humans, brands have a character. Like us, they need to have a style, a dressing sense, and a style of communication to grab people's attention. In this book, we'll get into the depth of each of the brand assets from brand name, story, logo, colors, typography, tone of voice, imagery, iconography, illustrations to compiling them in a holy brand style guide. It'll be an exciting journey.

If you're a brand strategist, marketer, brand agency team member, at a manager post, a business owner, or an entrepreneur looking to establish your business as a brand, this is for you. If you're a young design or business graduate struggling to understand the practical applications of your theory classes in Branding and Marketing, this is for you. If you're a 9-5 stuck employee at a stressful job and willing to set up your own business or brand but don't have the capital to invest in building your brand, this will help you construct it.

In the last book, 'BYOB Building Your Own Brand', we talked about the first steps towards creating a brand strategy, value proposition statement, brand character, and the various types of brand logos. This book is a continuation of where we left in the last book. Although you can read it without going through the previous book, I would recommend you to read it too if you wish to gain a better foundation in brand building. Here we will understand what a particular brand asset is used for, how it needs to be created, where it should be used, and how to make it a successful brand asset that evokes a strong brand recall in the minds of your audience.

All the chapters are supported by examples from brands all over the world. The last chapter focuses on compiling the valuable brand assets in the form of a style guide with guidelines, descriptions, information, standards, best practices, do's and don'ts, and instructions for anyone who will be involved in brand building exercises.

A strong visual identity is the need for a modern brand to evolve in this digital era and a necessity for a legacy brand to continue growing business. Over 90% of businesses around the world today depend on highly aesthetical and meaningful visual communication. How do we achieve this? With all the visual and emotional clutter filling the digital space and no one really looking at your advertisements anymore? How do we attract people and hook them to your brand?

We do it by providing them value. Value through an exclusive visual means of communication. Obviously, there's something particular about how your brand dresses up to perform in front of your audience. These accessories it wears are your brand's assets and, in this book, you'll discover how to make them.

About The Author

Karan Gupta

Karan Gupta is an architect from the School of Planning and Architecture, Bhopal, India; worked as a communication designer in architecture firms establishing their brands through branding strategy, brand assets, and public relations. He spent six months in a French medieval town as an architecture intern during which he traveled across twenty towns and cities across Europe by road. His architecture and communications experience in France expanded his horizons to explore branding for designers who struggle to market themselves and their works. He has an utter disregard for conventional pedagogy and a passion for revolutionary archetypes.

www.ingramcontent.com/pod-product-compliance
Lightning Source LLC
Chambersburg PA
CBHW031632210526
45464CB00004B/1855